# Modern Family Mad Libs

by Pieta Pemberton

PRICE STERN SLOAN
An imprint of Penguin Random House LLC

Mad Libs format copyright © 2016 by Price Stern Sloan,
an imprint of Penguin Random House LLC. All rights reserved.

Concept created by Roger Price and Leonard Stern.

Modern Family TM & © 2016 Twentieth Century Fox Film Corporation. All rights reserved.

Published by Price Stern Sloan,
an imprint of Penguin Random House LLC,
345 Hudson Street, New York, New York 10014.
Printed in the USA.

Penguin supports copyright. Copyright fuels creativity, encourages diverse voices, promotes free speech, and creates a vibrant culture. Thank you for buying an authorized edition of this book and for complying with copyright laws by not reproducing, scanning, or distributing any part of it in any form without permission. You are supporting writers and allowing Penguin to continue to publish books for every reader.

ISBN 978-0-8431-8307-8

13 5 7 9 10 8 6 4 2

PSS!, MAD LIBS, and ADULT MAD LIBS are registered trademarks of Penguin Random House LLC.

# INSTRUCTIONS

MAD LIBS® is a game for people who don't like games! It can be played by one, two, three, four, or forty.

## • RIDICULOUSLY SIMPLE DIRECTIONS

In this book, you'll find stories containing blank spaces where words are left out. One player, the READER, selects one of the stories. The READER shouldn't tell anyone what the story is about. Instead, the READER should ask the other players, the WRITERS, to give words to fill in the blank spaces in the story.

## • TO PLAY

The READER asks each WRITER in turn to call out words—adjectives or nouns or whatever the spaces call for—and uses them to fill in the blank spaces in the story. The result is your very own MAD LIBS! Then, when the READER reads the completed MAD LIBS to the other players, they will discover they have written a story that is fantastic, screamingly funny, shocking, silly, crazy, or just plain dumb—depending on the words each WRITER called out.

## • EXAMPLE (*Before* and *After*)

"_____!" he said _____
    EXCLAMATION                    ADVERB

as he jumped into his convertible _____ and
                                        NOUN

drove off with his _____ wife.
                      ADJECTIVE

"*Ouch*!" he said *stupidly*
  EXCLAMATION            ADVERB

as he jumped into his convertible *cat* and
                                  NOUN

drove off with his *brave* wife.
                 ADJECTIVE

# QUICK REVIEW

In case you have forgotten what adjectives, adverbs, nouns, and verbs are, here is a quick review:

An **ADJECTIVE** describes something or somebody. *Lumpy, soft, ugly, messy,* and *short* are adjectives.

An **ADVERB** tells how something is done. It modifies a verb and usually ends in "ly." *Modestly, stupidly, greedily,* and *carefully* are adverbs.

A **NOUN** is the name of a person, place, or thing. *Sidewalk, umbrella, bridle, bathtub,* and *nose* are nouns.

A **VERB** is an action word. *Run, pitch, jump,* and *swim* are verbs. Put the verbs in past tense if the directions say **PAST TENSE**. *Ran, pitched, jumped,* and *swam* are verbs in the past tense.

When we ask for **A PLACE**, we mean any sort of place: a country or city (*Spain, Cleveland*) or a room (*bathroom, kitchen*).

An **EXCLAMATION** or **SILLY WORD** is any sort of funny sound, gasp, grunt, or outcry, like *Wow!, Ouch!, Whomp!, Ick!,* and *Gadzooks!*

When we ask for specific words, like a **NUMBER**, a **COLOR**, an **ANIMAL**, or a **PART OF THE BODY**, we mean a word that is one of those things, like *seven, blue, horse,* or *head*.

When we ask for a **PLURAL**, it means more than one. For example, *cat* pluralized is *cats*.

# WHO IN THE MODERN FAMILY ARE YOU?

MAD LIBS® is fun to play with friends, but you can also play it by yourself! To begin with, DO NOT look at the story on the page below. Fill in the blanks on this page with the words called for. Then, using the words you have selected, fill in the blank spaces in the story. Now you've created your own hilarious MAD LIBS® game!

ADJECTIVE ___beautiful___

PLURAL NOUN ___people___

ADJECTIVE ___Hot___

A PLACE ___diner___

OCCUPATION (PLURAL) ___Financial advisor___

NOUN ___Pig___

VERB ___Ran___

ADJECTIVE ___expensive___

NOUN ___dog___

VERB ENDING IN "ING" ___Running___

NOUN ___Movie theater___

NOUN ___daughter___

ADJECTIVE ___Silly___

# WHO IN THE MODERN FAMILY ARE YOU?

Do you love fashion, __beautiful__ (ADJECTIVE) clothes, and high-heeled __people__ (PLURAL NOUN)? You could be just like Gloria or Haley, the __hot__ (ADJECTIVE) queens. Or are you more sophisticated—enjoying afternoons at (the) __diner__ (A PLACE) talking about the most famous __financial advisors__ (OCCUPATION (PLURAL)) of the eighteenth century? What a/an __pig__ (NOUN)—you'd easily fit right in with Alex, Manny, and Mitch. Maybe you're more of a/an __run__ (VERB)-it-all who needs to be __expensive__ (ADJECTIVE) about everything—just like Claire and Jay. If you like to be a/an __dog__ (NOUN)-ball and are always __running__ (VERB ENDING IN "ING") around, you're probably similar to Luke and his __movie theatre__ (NOUN), Phil. But if you're a drama __daughter__ (NOUN) and you want everything to be absolutely __silly__ (ADJECTIVE), well, *hellooo*, Cam and Lily!

From ADULT MAD LIBS®: Modern Family Mad Libs • TM & © 2016 Twentieth Century Fox Film Corporation. Published by Price Stern Sloan, an imprint of Penguin Random House LLC, 345 Hudson Street, New York, NY 10014.

## MANNY IN LOVE

MAD LIBS® is fun to play with friends, but you can also play it by yourself! To begin with, DO NOT look at the story on the page below. Fill in the blanks on this page with the words called for. Then, using the words you have selected, fill in the blank spaces in the story. Now you've created your own hilarious MAD LIBS® game!

ADJECTIVE _____

NOUN _____

ADVERB _____

VERB ENDING IN "ING" _____

NOUN _____

NUMBER _____

ADJECTIVE _____

NOUN _____

PART OF THE BODY (PLURAL) _____

ADJECTIVE _____

VERB _____

NOUN _____

PLURAL NOUN _____

VERB _____

NOUN _____

PART OF THE BODY _____

VERB _____

# MANNY IN LOVE

Oh, Manny. He's such a/an _____ , sweet young _____ .
                          ADJECTIVE                        NOUN
No matter how _____ he tries, Manny just can't stop
                 ADVERB
_____ for almost every _____ he meets. It
VERB ENDING IN "ING"              NOUN
doesn't matter if they are _____ years older than him, or in
                              NUMBER
the _____ group at school, or even related to him (not by
     ADJECTIVE
_____ , thankfully)! Manny falls in love with almost every
   NOUN
single girl he sets _____ on. Sometimes he will watch
                    PART OF THE BODY (PLURAL)
them from a/an _____ distance, never building up the
                  ADJECTIVE
courage to go _____ to them. Sometimes he'll write a love
                 VERB
_____ or pick them a bunch of _____ , but it never
   NOUN                                  PLURAL NOUN
works—they all _____ no. And when he finally did get a/an
                  VERB
_____ -friend, she just broke his _____ . Will
   NOUN                                     PART OF THE BODY
Manny ever find someone to _____ ?
                              VERB

### Adult MAD LIBS®
The world's greatest ~~family~~ game

# INSIDE MARRIAGE

MAD LIBS® is fun to play with friends, but you can also play it by yourself! To begin with, DO NOT look at the story on the page below. Fill in the blanks on this page with the words called for. Then, using the words you have selected, fill in the blank spaces in the story. Now you've created your own hilarious MAD LIBS® game!

ADJECTIVE _____

ADVERB _____

VERB _____

NOUN _____

VERB _____

PERSON IN ROOM (MALE) _____

PERSON IN ROOM (FEMALE) _____

NOUN _____

TYPE OF LIQUID (PLURAL) _____

NOUN _____

PLURAL NOUN _____

NOUN _____

PLURAL NOUN _____

NOUN _____

ADJECTIVE _____

ANIMAL (PLURAL) _____

NOUN _____

# INSIDE MARRIAGE

They say that marriage can be _____, and you have to
                                  ADJECTIVE
_____ work at it. This is certainly true, but Phil and Claire
   ADVERB
are both willing to make it _____. If they ever feel like they
                                 VERB
are losing their _____, they'll make sure they _____
                     NOUN                                      VERB
it up! Every February for _____'s Day, Phil and
                            PERSON IN ROOM (MALE)
Claire role-play as Clive and _____. They meet in a
                                PERSON IN ROOM (FEMALE)
hotel _____, order two _____ with a twist, and
          NOUN                     TYPE OF LIQUID (PLURAL)
see where the night takes them! For their _____ anniversary,
                                               NOUN
Phil likes to surprise Claire with heart-shaped _____, red
                                                   PLURAL NOUN
_____ petals, and sparkly _____. And Claire once
    NOUN                               PLURAL NOUN
hired a famous _____ player to put on a private concert at their
                   NOUN
house! It takes some _____ planning, but that's how these two
                         ADJECTIVE
love-_____ keep their _____ burning.
       ANIMAL (PLURAL)              NOUN

# PHIL'S GUIDE TO BEING A COOL DAD

MAD LIBS® is fun to play with friends, but you can also play it by yourself! To begin with, DO NOT look at the story on the page below. Fill in the blanks on this page with the words called for. Then, using the words you have selected, fill in the blank spaces in the story. Now you've created your own hilarious MAD LIBS® game!

ADJECTIVE _____

PLURAL NOUN _____

ADJECTIVE _____

NOUN _____

ADJECTIVE _____

PLURAL NOUN _____

NOUN _____

VERB _____

PLURAL NOUN _____

VERB ENDING IN "ING" _____

ADJECTIVE _____

VERB _____

ADVERB _____

# PHIL'S GUIDE TO BEING A COOL DAD

Being the _____ dad is Phil's "thing." He tries to talk to his
           ADJECTIVE

_____ on their level—he's all about keeping it _____.
PLURAL NOUN                                                ADJECTIVE

Here are a few pointers to help you be a cool _____, too:
                                                NOUN

- Use the same _____ words and phrases that your kids use.
                 ADJECTIVE

  If that means you have to eavesdrop on some of the conversations

  they have with their _____, that's okay. Just don't get
                       PLURAL NOUN

  caught!

- Always respect your kids' _____. They have to be able
                             NOUN

  to talk to you, and they won't do that if you don't _____
                                                       VERB

  their privacy.

- Be a friend to their _____. You can even call their friends
                       PLURAL NOUN

  sometimes, just to see what's _____.
                                VERB ENDING IN "ING"

- Most _____ of all: If you mess up, _____
        ADJECTIVE                                  VERB

  _____!
   ADVERB

From ADULT MAD LIBS®: Modern Family Mad Libs • TM & © 2016 Twentieth Century Fox Film
Corporation. Published by Price Stern Sloan, an imprint of Penguin Random House LLC,
345 Hudson Street, New York, NY 10014.

# ODE TO A BROKEN STAIR, BY THE BROKEN STAIR

MAD LIBS® is fun to play with friends, but you can also play it by yourself! To begin with, DO NOT look at the story on the page below. Fill in the blanks on this page with the words called for. Then, using the words you have selected, fill in the blank spaces in the story. Now you've created your own hilarious MAD LIBS® game!

NUMBER _____

NOUN _____

PART OF THE BODY (PLURAL) _____

CELEBRITY (FEMALE) _____

PLURAL NOUN _____

ADJECTIVE _____

VERB (PAST TENSE) _____

NOUN _____

NOUN _____

NOUN _____

ADJECTIVE _____

# ODE TO A BROKEN STAIR, BY THE BROKEN STAIR

As stair number _____ on the Dunphy family _____-
                    NUMBER                                          NOUN

case, it's my job to keep everybody on their _____.
                                              PART OF THE BODY (PLURAL)

One time, Phil was trying to convince his wife, _____,
                                                  CELEBRITY (FEMALE)

that he always finishes the _____ he has started. Just to prove
                             PLURAL NOUN

him _____, I pushed a few screws loose so he _____
       ADJECTIVE                                        VERB (PAST TENSE)

when he tried to step on me. Then, there was the time Claire wanted

to take a family _____ with everyone on the staircase. Seeing
                    NOUN

as I'm a little _____-shy, I had to make sure she couldn't
                   NOUN

fix me. My _____ worked, and they took the picture
              NOUN

outside instead! It's a/an _____ job, but someone has to do it.
                            ADJECTIVE

From ADULT MAD LIBS®: Modern Family Mad Libs • TM & © 2016 Twentieth Century Fox Film Corporation. Published by Price Stern Sloan, an imprint of Penguin Random House LLC, 345 Hudson Street, New York, NY 10014.

# Adult MAD LIBS
The world's greatest ~~family~~ game

# CREATIVE CAM

MAD LIBS® is fun to play with friends, but you can also play it by yourself! To begin with, DO NOT look at the story on the page below. Fill in the blanks on this page with the words called for. Then, using the words you have selected, fill in the blank spaces in the story. Now you've created your own hilarious MAD LIBS® game!

ADJECTIVE _____

NOUN _____

NOUN _____

PLURAL NOUN _____

PERSON IN ROOM (MALE) _____

VERB _____

ADJECTIVE _____

A PLACE _____

CELEBRITY (MALE) _____

VERB ENDING IN "ING" _____

PLURAL NOUN _____

ADJECTIVE _____

ADJECTIVE _____

NOUN _____

NUMBER _____

NUMBER _____

VERB ENDING IN "ING" _____

NOUN _____

# CREATIVE CAM

Whether it's a baptism, a/an _____ play, or just a Tuesday,
                                    ADJECTIVE
you can always count on Cam to add some creative _____!
                                                        NOUN
When his _____, Lily, was a baby, he used to dress her up as
              NOUN
famous _____ like Olivia Newton-John, Madonna, and
          PLURAL NOUN
_____ Wonder. And though he doesn't always _____
PERSON IN ROOM (MALE)                                           VERB
it, Cam is a/an _____ musician. He once even played at (the)
                    ADJECTIVE
_____ with _____'s band when they needed a
  A PLACE              CELEBRTIY (MALE)
drummer! He is excellent at _____, arranges perfect
                                  VERB ENDING IN "ING"
_____, and shoots _____ films. Though, really, one
PLURAL NOUN                    ADJECTIVE
of Cam's most _____ achievements was sewing a mermaid
                  ADJECTIVE
costume for a pet _____. With _____ beads and more
                        NOUN              NUMBER
than _____ hours of _____, it was truly a/an
        NUMBER                VERB ENDING IN "ING"
_____ of art!
    NOUN

# JAY, THE DAD

MAD LIBS® is fun to play with friends, but you can also play it by yourself! To begin with, DO NOT look at the story on the page below. Fill in the blanks on this page with the words called for. Then, using the words you have selected, fill in the blank spaces in the story. Now you've created your own hilarious MAD LIBS® game!

NOUN _____

CELEBRITY (MALE) _____

CELEBRITY (FEMALE) _____

PLURAL NOUN _____

PLURAL NOUN _____

ADJECTIVE _____

VERB ENDING IN "ING" _____

PERSON IN ROOM (FEMALE) _____

PERSON IN ROOM (MALE) _____

PLURAL NOUN _____

ADJECTIVE _____

NUMBER _____

NOUN _____

PLURAL NOUN _____

ADJECTIVE _____

ADJECTIVE _____

# JAY, THE DAD

Jay was never really made for _____-hood. When his kids,
                                   NOUN

_____ and _____, were young, he wasn't around—
CELEBRITY (MALE)   CELEBRITY (FEMALE)

he was too busy building his company, Pritchett's _____ &
                                                    PLURAL NOUN

_____. His kids always thought that he was too _____
PLURAL NOUN                                              ADJECTIVE

on them, but he still says it was for _____ character!
                                      VERB ENDING IN "ING"

But when Jay married _____ and became a stepfather
                     PERSON IN ROOM (FEMALE)

to _____, he softened a little bit. He tried to protect
   PERSON IN ROOM (MALE)

Manny's _____ a lot more, and was supportive when Manny
        PLURAL NOUN

was _____. By the time Jay had another baby, he was
    ADJECTIVE

_____ years old and actually excited to be a/an _____
NUMBER                                                  NOUN

again. Though it was lucky he had so many _____ around to
                                           PLURAL NOUN

help him! As Jay learned, being a father is _____ at any age, but
                                            ADJECTIVE

it's also just as _____.
                  ADJECTIVE

From ADULT MAD LIBS®: Modern Family Mad Libs • TM & © 2016 Twentieth Century Fox Film
Corporation. Published by Price Stern Sloan, an imprint of Penguin Random House LLC,
345 Hudson Street, New York, NY 10014.

# GLORIA

MAD LIBS® is fun to play with friends, but you can also play it by yourself! To begin with, DO NOT look at the story on the page below. Fill in the blanks on this page with the words called for. Then, using the words you have selected, fill in the blank spaces in the story. Now you've created your own hilarious MAD LIBS® game!

ADJECTIVE _____

NOUN _____

PLURAL NOUN _____

A PLACE _____

NOUN _____

ADJECTIVE _____

PERSON IN ROOM (FEMALE) _____

NOUN _____

CELEBRITY (MALE) _____

NUMBER _____

NOUN _____

A PLACE _____

VERB _____

NOUN _____

ADJECTIVE _____

NOUN _____

PERSON IN ROOM (MALE) _____

# GLORIA

Sure, she has a/an _____ husband, a beautiful _____,
                    ADJECTIVE                              NOUN

and more _____ than ever before, but life hasn't always been this
          PLURAL NOUN

way for Gloria. Back in her hometown of (the) _____ (which
                                                A PLACE

happens to be the _____ of Colombia!), Gloria's babysitter was
                      NOUN

a/an _____ goat named _____. When Gloria
       ADJECTIVE                  PERSON IN ROOM (FEMALE)

split up with her ex-_____, she took her son, _____,
                        NOUN                             CELEBRITY (MALE)

and moved to a small _____-bedroom _____ in (the)
                         NUMBER                  NOUN

_____. To help make ends _____, she became a/an
  A PLACE                             VERB

_____ driver, driving a/an _____ taxi around the city
    NOUN                              ADJECTIVE

while Manny slept in the back-_____. It took some time before
                                  NOUN

she met _____, but once she did, she never looked back.
         PERSON IN ROOM (MALE)

From ADULT MAD LIBS®: Modern Family Mad Libs • TM & © 2016 Twentieth Century Fox Film
Corporation. Published by Price Stern Sloan, an imprint of Penguin Random House LLC,
345 Hudson Street, New York, NY 10014.

# TIPS FOR YOUR DREAM WEDDING

MAD LIBS® is fun to play with friends, but you can also play it by yourself! To begin with, DO NOT look at the story on the page below. Fill in the blanks on this page with the words called for. Then, using the words you have selected, fill in the blank spaces in the story. Now you've created your own hilarious MAD LIBS® game!

ADJECTIVE _____

NOUN _____

NOUN _____

NOUN _____

ADJECTIVE _____

ARTICLE OF CLOTHING _____

NOUN _____

ADJECTIVE _____

NOUN _____

VERB _____

PLURAL NOUN _____

A PLACE _____

NOUN _____

NUMBER _____

ADJECTIVE _____

VERB _____

NOUN _____

# TIPS FOR YOUR DREAM WEDDING

Trying to plan your _____ wedding? Take a leaf out of Mitch
                       ADJECTIVE

and Cam's _____ and plan everything down to the last tiny
               NOUN

_____! Here are some tips to stop things from going wrong:
    NOUN

- Pick up your _____ from the dry cleaner a day early.
                     NOUN

   Otherwise, the _____ cleaner may be closed and you won't
                        ADJECTIVE

   have a/an _____ to wear!
                  ARTICLE OF CLOTHING

- Avoid wildfires at all costs. A wild-_____ will certainly
                                              NOUN

   ruin an otherwise _____ day.
                           ADJECTIVE

- Make sure that the parents of the _____ aren't fighting
                                              NOUN

   with each other. And especially don't let them _____ from
                                                         VERB

   your secret flask!

- If your venue is evacuated by _____, stay calm. You can
                                       PLURAL NOUN

   always find another venue, even if it is just (the) _____.
                                                              A PLACE

- Don't let a/an _____ who is _____ months
                       NOUN                    NUMBER

   pregnant officiate the wedding.

- Finally, and most importantly, if it all goes _____, try to
                                                       ADJECTIVE

   _____ about it with the _____ you love.
        VERB                              NOUN

From ADULT MAD LIBS®: Modern Family Mad Libs • TM & © 2016 Twentieth Century Fox Film
Corporation. Published by Price Stern Sloan, an imprint of Penguin Random House LLC,
345 Hudson Street, New York, NY 10014.

## Adult MAD LIBS
The world's greatest _family_ game

# LIFE OF LILY

MAD LIBS® is fun to play with friends, but you can also play it by yourself! To begin with, DO NOT look at the story on the page below. Fill in the blanks on this page with the words called for. Then, using the words you have selected, fill in the blank spaces in the story. Now you've created your own hilarious MAD LIBS® game!

NOUN _____

A PLACE _____

ADJECTIVE _____

ADJECTIVE _____

PERSON IN ROOM (MALE) _____

PERSON IN ROOM (MALE) _____

VERB ENDING IN "ING" _____

A PLACE _____

PLURAL NOUN _____

ADJECTIVE _____

VERB _____

ADJECTIVE _____

PLURAL NOUN _____

NOUN _____

NOUN _____

NOUN _____

PERSON IN ROOM (MALE) _____

ADJECTIVE _____

# LIFE OF LILY

I first met Lily when she was just a tiny _____ in (the)
                                              NOUN

_____. She was such a/an _____ baby, and she
   A PLACE                              ADJECTIVE

deserved a/an _____ life. When _____ and
                 ADJECTIVE                    PERSON IN ROOM (MALE)

_____ came to pick her up from the orphanage, she was
PERSON IN ROOM (MALE)

so happy she couldn't stop _____! It didn't take her long to
                             VERB ENDING IN "ING"

adjust to life in (the) _____. Her two _____ loved
                           A PLACE                       PLURAL NOUN

her so much—they were _____ parents from the start. They
                          ADJECTIVE

taught her how to _____ and when to be _____, and
                      VERB                              ADJECTIVE

they bought her lots of beautiful _____. They even built her
                                      PLURAL NOUN

a/an _____, complete with turrets and a drawbridge! She
        NOUN

could dress up and feel like a/an _____. For a little while,
                                       NOUN

her dads were going to adopt another _____, but when that
                                          NOUN

didn't work out, they got Lily a pet cat named _____
                                                  PERSON IN ROOM (MALE)

instead. To be honest, I think Lily was more _____ this way!
                                                 ADJECTIVE

From ADULT MAD LIBS®: Modern Family Mad Libs • TM & © 2016 Twentieth Century Fox Film
Corporation. Published by Price Stern Sloan, an imprint of Penguin Random House LLC,
345 Hudson Street, New York, NY 10014.

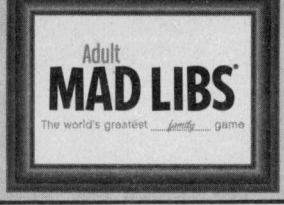

# GROWING UP WITH MITCH

MAD LIBS® is fun to play with friends, but you can also play it by yourself! To begin with, DO NOT look at the story on the page below. Fill in the blanks on this page with the words called for. Then, using the words you have selected, fill in the blank spaces in the story. Now you've created your own hilarious MAD LIBS® game!

NOUN _____

ADJECTIVE _____

OCCUPATION _____

CELEBRITY (MALE) _____

NOUN _____

ADJECTIVE _____

NOUN _____

SAME NOUN _____

NOUN _____

VERB ENDING IN "ING" _____

PLURAL NOUN _____

NOUN _____

VERB _____

PERSON IN ROOM (FEMALE) _____

NOUN _____

VERB _____

NOUN _____

NOUN _____

# GROWING UP WITH MITCH

Mitch really has his _____ together now, but he had a
                        NOUN
pretty _____ time growing up. Before he became a/an
        ADJECTIVE
_____, and long before he met _____ and
  OCCUPATION                              CELEBRITY (MALE)
adopted his _____, he was just a/an _____,
               NOUN                              ADJECTIVE
quiet young _____ trying to find his way. Being a shy
               NOUN
_____, he spent a lot of time inside, playing with his pet
  SAME NOUN
_____ or _____ to musicals all day long. He wasn't
  NOUN            VERB ENDING IN "ING"
ever interested in watching _____ with his dad—something
                              PLURAL NOUN
his _____ could never understand! Though he did love to
     NOUN
figure-_____ with his sister, _____, in their skating
         VERB                          PERSON IN ROOM (FEMALE)
duo called Fire and _____. He couldn't _____ a ball or
                      NOUN                         VERB
hammer a/an _____, but he knew he would never need those
               NOUN
skills if he fulfilled his dream of being a professional _____!
                                                          NOUN

From ADULT MAD LIBS®: Modern Family Mad Libs • TM & © 2016 Twentieth Century Fox Film
Corporation. Published by Price Stern Sloan, an imprint of Penguin Random House LLC,
345 Hudson Street, New York, NY 10014.

# GROWING UP WITH CLAIRE

MAD LIBS® is fun to play with friends, but you can also play it by yourself! To begin with, DO NOT look at the story on the page below. Fill in the blanks on this page with the words called for. Then, using the words you have selected, fill in the blank spaces in the story. Now you've created your own hilarious MAD LIBS® game!

NOUN _____

NOUN _____

VERB ENDING IN "ING" _____

A PLACE _____

VERB ENDING IN "ING" _____

TYPE OF LIQUID _____

NOUN _____

VERB (PAST TENSE) _____

VERB ENDING IN "ING" _____

ADJECTIVE _____

NOUN _____

PERSON IN ROOM (MALE) _____

VERB _____

ADJECTIVE _____

NOUN _____

NOUN _____

# GROWING UP WITH CLAIRE

We know Claire as a loving and responsible _____, but
                                              NOUN
when she was younger she was a bit of a wild _____! She was
                                              NOUN
always _____ out at night to go to (the) _____
       VERB ENDING IN "ING"                           A PLACE
with her boyfriend, or _____ so much _____ that
                       VERB ENDING IN "ING"          TYPE OF LIQUID
she would wake up with a terrible _____. Once, she even
                                   NOUN
_____ out in the car after _____ too hard!
VERB (PAST TENSE)                       VERB ENDING IN "ING"
She was always very _____—the opposite of her younger
                    ADJECTIVE
_____, _____—and hated being told what
NOUN            PERSON IN ROOM (MALE)
to do. She did things her own way, no matter what anyone else
would _____! And even though she could be a little bit
      VERB
_____, she always did it out of _____. That's just the
ADJECTIVE                                  NOUN
kind of caring _____ she is.
               NOUN

From ADULT MAD LIBS®: Modern Family Mad Libs • TM & © 2016 Twentieth Century Fox Film
Corporation. Published by Price Stern Sloan, an imprint of Penguin Random House LLC,
345 Hudson Street, New York, NY 10014.

# DYLAN THE MUSIC MAN

MAD LIBS® is fun to play with friends, but you can also play it by yourself! To begin with, DO NOT look at the story on the page below. Fill in the blanks on this page with the words called for. Then, using the words you have selected, fill in the blank spaces in the story. Now you've created your own hilarious MAD LIBS® game!

VERB ENDING IN "ING" _____

NOUN _____

NUMBER _____

NOUN _____

PLURAL NOUN _____

ADJECTIVE _____

PLURAL NOUN _____

PART OF THE BODY _____

PLURAL NOUN _____

ADJECTIVE _____

NOUN _____

NOUN _____

VERB _____

SAME VERB _____

NOUN _____

CELEBRITY (MALE) _____

VERB _____

# DYLAN THE MUSIC MAN

You may not know it from _____ at him, but Dylan is
                        VERB ENDING IN "ING"
actually a very talented _____! When he was just _____
                            NOUN                            NUMBER
years old, he picked up an old _____ and started teaching himself
                                  NOUN
how to play it. First he learned a few of the most basic _____,
                                                          PLURAL NOUN
then he moved on to the more _____ chords. Once he had
                               ADJECTIVE
mastered those _____, he decided to try his _____
                PLURAL NOUN                        PART OF THE BODY
at writing _____. Here is part of one of his most _____
            PLURAL NOUN                                  ADJECTIVE
songs, written for his _____, Haley:
                         NOUN

'Cause maybe, _____, I just wanna do you, do you.
                NOUN

Do you wanna _____ me, _____ me
              VERB              SAME VERB

underneath the _____-light,
                  NOUN

the moonlight tonight?

He may not be _____, but he sure can make a girl
                CELEBRITY (MALE)
_____!
  VERB

From ADULT MAD LIBS®: Modern Family Mad Libs • TM & © 2016 Twentieth Century Fox Film
Corporation. Published by Price Stern Sloan, an imprint of Penguin Random House LLC,
345 Hudson Street, New York, NY 10014.

# MOVING ON WITH DEDE

MAD LIBS® is fun to play with friends, but you can also play it by yourself! To begin with, DO NOT look at the story on the page below. Fill in the blanks on this page with the words called for. Then, using the words you have selected, fill in the blank spaces in the story. Now you've created your own hilarious MAD LIBS® game!

VERB ENDING IN "ING" _____

NOUN _____

NOUN _____

ADJECTIVE _____

A PLACE _____

ADJECTIVE _____

CELEBRITY (FEMALE) _____

ADJECTIVE _____

NUMBER _____

ADJECTIVE _____

ADJECTIVE _____

PERSON IN ROOM (MALE) _____

NOUN _____

NOUN _____

ADJECTIVE _____

VERB _____

SILLY WORD _____

# MOVING ON WITH DEDE

After _____ her thirty-five-year marriage with Jay, DeDe is
         VERB ENDING IN "ING"

finally moving on with her _____. You may think that her
                            NOUN

ex-_____ finding a young, stunningly _____ woman
     NOUN                                      ADJECTIVE

from (the) _____ to marry would bother her a little bit,
             A PLACE

but DeDe is totally _____ with it! Yes, Jay married
                      ADJECTIVE

_____ only a short time after he and DeDe got divorced,
 CELEBRITY (FEMALE)

but that doesn't bother DeDe at all. And sure, Gloria makes Jay

more _____ than he has been in _____ years, but
      ADJECTIVE                            NUMBER

do you think DeDe is _____ about it? No way. She is so
                      ADJECTIVE

much more _____ now than she has ever been. She has a
            ADJECTIVE

new man, _____, and she practices _____ every
          PERSON IN ROOM (MALE)              NOUN

morning. She talks to her _____ weekly, and her life will
                           NOUN

soon be _____—once she can _____ that Colombian
         ADJECTIVE                     VERB

_____ who ruined her life!
 SILLY WORD

From ADULT MAD LIBS®: Modern Family Mad Libs • TM & © 2016 Twentieth Century Fox Film
Corporation. Published by Price Stern Sloan, an imprint of Penguin Random House LLC,
345 Hudson Street, New York, NY 10014.

# THE LUKE OF THE FAMILY

MAD LIBS® is fun to play with friends, but you can also play it by yourself! To begin with, DO NOT look at the story on the page below. Fill in the blanks on this page with the words called for. Then, using the words you have selected, fill in the blank spaces in the story. Now you've created your own hilarious MAD LIBS® game!

NOUN _____

SAME NOUN _____

PART OF THE BODY _____

ADJECTIVE _____

ARTICLE OF CLOTHING (PLURAL) _____

PLURAL NOUN _____

VERB ENDING IN "ING" _____

ADJECTIVE _____

ADJECTIVE _____

PLURAL NOUN _____

NOUN _____

ADJECTIVE _____

NOUN _____

PLURAL NOUN _____

VERB _____

VERB _____

# THE LUKE OF THE FAMILY

Luke has never really been the sharpest _____ in the
                                         NOUN

_____-box. For example, he frequently gets his _____
  SAME NOUN                                              PART OF THE BODY

stuck in the banister, doesn't understand _____ words, and
                                             ADJECTIVE

he never used to wear any _____—but he still has
                          ARTICLE OF CLOTHING (PLURAL)

some great _____. For instance, he loves _____
            PLURAL NOUN                              VERB ENDING IN "ING"

movies and has even starred in his own movie about zombies in a

post-_____ wasteland. It was really _____! He also
      ADJECTIVE                               ADJECTIVE

loves playing _____ on people. Sometimes it works out,
               PLURAL NOUN

though sometimes it is a complete _____ and everyone gets
                                     NOUN

really _____ at him. But perhaps Luke's best _____
        ADJECTIVE                                        NOUN

is how much he loves his _____ and sisters. He tries to
                          PLURAL NOUN

_____ it sometimes, but there is nothing he wouldn't
   VERB

_____ for them!
   VERB

From ADULT MAD LIBS®: Modern Family Mad Libs • TM & © 2016 Twentieth Century Fox Film
Corporation. Published by Price Stern Sloan, an imprint of Penguin Random House LLC,
345 Hudson Street, New York, NY 10014.

# THE DINNER PARTY, PART 1

MAD LIBS® is fun to play with friends, but you can also play it by yourself! To begin with, DO NOT look at the story on the page below. Fill in the blanks on this page with the words called for. Then, using the words you have selected, fill in the blank spaces in the story. Now you've created your own hilarious MAD LIBS® game!

PLURAL NOUN _____

ADJECTIVE _____

VERB _____

NOUN _____

NOUN _____

ADJECTIVE _____

NOUN _____

NUMBER _____

NOUN _____

VERB _____

TYPE OF LIQUID _____

VERB ENDING IN "ING" _____

NOUN _____

PLURAL NOUN _____

ADJECTIVE _____

VERB _____

NOUN _____

ADJECTIVE _____

# THE DINNER PARTY, PART 1

Like most _____, the Dunphy-Pritchett-Tucker-Delgado
            PLURAL NOUN
family loves to celebrate _____ occasions. And what better
                          ADJECTIVE
way to _____ a special _____ than with a dinner party!
         VERB                      NOUN
The only problem with _____ parties is that they can be more
                        NOUN
_____ than you might think. The host has the most work to
 ADJECTIVE
do—the _____ needs to be stuffed and cooked for _____
         NOUN                                                NUMBER
hours, the _____ needs to be cleaned, someone needs to
             NOUN
_____ the table, and most importantly, _____ needs to
 VERB                                             TYPE OF LIQUID
be bought! Meanwhile, the other families are _____ around
                                               VERB ENDING IN "ING"
trying to do everything they need to do before the _____
                                                      NOUN
starts—pick out a nice bouquet of _____, make a/an
                                    PLURAL NOUN
_____ dessert, and, most importantly for them, decide what
 ADJECTIVE
to _____. By the time the dinner _____ actually starts,
    VERB                                   NOUN
everyone is feeling completely _____!
                                 ADJECTIVE

# THE DINNER PARTY, PART 2

MAD LIBS® is fun to play with friends, but you can also play it by yourself! To begin with, DO NOT look at the story on the page below. Fill in the blanks on this page with the words called for. Then, using the words you have selected, fill in the blank spaces in the story. Now you've created your own hilarious MAD LIBS® game!

PLURAL NOUN _____

NOUN _____

ADJECTIVE _____

VERB ENDING IN "ING" _____

ADVERB _____

ADVERB _____

NOUN _____

PART OF THE BODY (PLURAL) _____

TYPE OF FOOD _____

ANIMAL _____

NOUN _____

NOUN _____

PERSON IN ROOM (MALE) _____

SILLY WORD _____

ADJECTIVE _____

SILLY WORD _____

ADJECTIVE _____

# THE DINNER PARTY, PART 2

After all of that hard work, it's so nice to finally sit down and enjoy one another's company. That is, until all of the _____ start! One person breaks a/an _____ and has to quickly clean it up,
PLURAL NOUN                                                                                                    NOUN
while someone else says the food tastes a little _____. The host starts _____ _____, while the others just try to
                                                                              ADJECTIVE                       VERB ENDING IN "ING"   ADVERB
_____ eat their dinners. Then one of the kids falls off their
ADVERB
_____, another puts their _____ in the bowl of
NOUN                                                 PART OF THE BODY (PLURAL)
_____, the _____ starts barking at the _____,
TYPE OF FOOD               ANIMAL                                                       NOUN
and before you know it, the whole table erupts into a/an _____!
                                                                                                              NOUN
That's when _____ stands up and shouts, "_____!"
                     PERSON IN ROOM (MALE)                                          SILLY WORD
and everyone falls silent. They all realize they were being very
_____, and say "_____" to one another. It may seem
ADJECTIVE                       SILLY WORD
_____, but it's what family is all about.
ADJECTIVE

From ADULT MAD LIBS®: Modern Family Mad Libs • TM & © 2016 Twentieth Century Fox Film Corporation. Published by Price Stern Sloan, an imprint of Penguin Random House LLC, 345 Hudson Street, New York, NY 10014.

# HALEY'S DIARY

MAD LIBS® is fun to play with friends, but you can also play it by yourself! To begin with, DO NOT look at the story on the page below. Fill in the blanks on this page with the words called for. Then, using the words you have selected, fill in the blank spaces in the story. Now you've created your own hilarious MAD LIBS® game!

ADJECTIVE _____

ADJECTIVE _____

ADJECTIVE _____

NOUN _____

A PLACE _____

VERB ENDING IN "ING" _____

ADJECTIVE _____

PLURAL NOUN _____

ADJECTIVE _____

ADJECTIVE _____

NOUN _____

PLURAL NOUN _____

ADJECTIVE _____

NOUN _____

ADJECTIVE _____

VERB _____

# HALEY'S DIARY

I know it's not _____ to break into someone's diary, but I
                    ADJECTIVE
just couldn't help myself! Haley Dunphy is so _____, and
                                                ADJECTIVE
the temptation was too much to resist. And, I found out some *pretty*
_____ things about this young _____. Did you
  ADJECTIVE                                  NOUN
know that she was kicked out of (the) _____ and arrested for
                                         A PLACE
underage _____? Not only that, but she felt _____
          VERB ENDING IN "ING"                              ADJECTIVE
about it! I think she did it just to annoy her _____. Although,
                                                 PLURAL NOUN
even though she makes it seem like she is really _____, she's
                                                    ADJECTIVE
actually a lot more _____ than you'd think. Underneath all
                      ADJECTIVE
that _____ and all those _____, all she wants is for
       NOUN                            PLURAL NOUN
her family to be _____ and for a/an _____ to treat her
                   ADJECTIVE                      NOUN
with the _____ respect she deserves. She may talk the talk, but
           ADJECTIVE
she doesn't _____ the walk!
              VERB

**Adult MAD LIBS**
The world's greatest _family_ game

# MANNY'S FATHER

MAD LIBS® is fun to play with friends, but you can also play it by yourself! To begin with, DO NOT look at the story on the page below. Fill in the blanks on this page with the words called for. Then, using the words you have selected, fill in the blank spaces in the story. Now you've created your own hilarious MAD LIBS® game!

NOUN _____

ADJECTIVE _____

PART OF THE BODY _____

ANIMAL (PLURAL) _____

PLURAL NOUN _____

NOUN _____

ADJECTIVE _____

NOUN _____

PLURAL NOUN _____

NOUN _____

VERB _____

ADJECTIVE _____

PLURAL NOUN _____

VERB _____

NOUN _____

ADJECTIVE _____

NOUN _____

# MANNY'S FATHER

Manny has always looked up to his _____. To him, his
NOUN

father is _____—he laughs in the _____ of fear! He
ADJECTIVE                                PART OF THE BODY

has wrestled _____ and jumped out of _____, and he
                ANIMAL (PLURAL)                           PLURAL NOUN

even rides a/an _____! But there are some things that Manny
                        NOUN

doesn't know. Despite all his charm, Javier is really very _____.
                                                                ADJECTIVE

He uses his _____ and good looks to lure _____ in,
                    NOUN                                         PLURAL NOUN

but then he never sticks around. He once promised to take Manny

to _____-land, but when the time came, he didn't even
        NOUN

_____ up! Javier was never a/an _____ husband to
    VERB                                                ADJECTIVE

Gloria, either. Their marriage was full of _____, and all they
                                                    PLURAL NOUN

did was _____, but he just wasn't a supportive _____
                VERB                                                    NOUN

for her. He is a/an _____ man, but he'll always be Manny's
                            ADJECTIVE

_____.
    NOUN

From ADULT MAD LIBS®: Modern Family Mad Libs • TM & © 2016 Twentieth Century Fox Film
Corporation. Published by Price Stern Sloan, an imprint of Penguin Random House LLC,
345 Hudson Street, New York, NY 10014.

# ALEX DUNPHY, FUTURE PRESIDENT

MAD LIBS® is fun to play with friends, but you can also play it by yourself! To begin with, DO NOT look at the story on the page below. Fill in the blanks on this page with the words called for. Then, using the words you have selected, fill in the blank spaces in the story. Now you've created your own hilarious MAD LIBS® game!

NOUN _____

ADJECTIVE _____

ADJECTIVE _____

NOUN _____

ADJECTIVE _____

PART OF THE BODY (PLURAL) _____

ARTICLE OF CLOTHING (PLURAL) _____

ADJECTIVE _____

NOUN _____

PART OF THE BODY _____

PLURAL NOUN _____

VERB _____

VERB ENDING IN "ING" _____

NUMBER _____

VERB ENDING IN "ING" _____

PLURAL NOUN _____

ADJECTIVE _____

# ALEX DUNPHY, FUTURE PRESIDENT

Alex Dunphy is the love of my _____! She is beautiful,
                                    NOUN

_____, and _____. I know that one day she could
 ADJECTIVE           ADJECTIVE

be the _____ of our country. A stunningly _____
        NOUN                                           ADJECTIVE

president, that is. Just look at the way her hair falls over her

_____, and her _____ make her
 PART OF THE BODY (PLURAL)         ARTICLE OF CLOTHING (PLURAL)

eyes look even bigger and more _____ than they already
                                ADJECTIVE

are. With her quick _____ and sharp _____, Alex
                     NOUN                    PART OF THE BODY

is surrounded by a bunch of _____ in that family of hers! I
                             PLURAL NOUN

know they mean well, but they just don't _____ her the way
                                          VERB

I do. While she works hard, _____ for _____
                             VERB ENDING IN "ING"      NUMBER

hours every day, they are usually just _____ or talking
                                        VERB ENDING IN "ING"

about _____. Sometimes I think they don't know how
       PLURAL NOUN

_____ they are to have her.
 ADJECTIVE

From ADULT MAD LIBS®: Modern Family Mad Libs • TM & © 2016 Twentieth Century Fox Film
Corporation. Published by Price Stern Sloan, an imprint of Penguin Random House LLC,
345 Hudson Street, New York, NY 10014.

# A DOG'S-EYE VIEW

MAD LIBS® is fun to play with friends, but you can also play it by yourself! To begin with, DO NOT look at the story on the page below. Fill in the blanks on this page with the words called for. Then, using the words you have selected, fill in the blank spaces in the story. Now you've created your own hilarious MAD LIBS® game!

NOUN _____

ADJECTIVE _____

NOUN _____

PLURAL NOUN _____

PLURAL NOUN _____

A PLACE _____

PERSON IN ROOM (MALE) _____

VERB _____

VERB _____

ADJECTIVE _____

PART OF THE BODY (PLURAL) _____

VERB _____

PERSON IN ROOM (FEMALE) _____

NOUN _____

NOUN _____

NOUN _____

# A DOG'S-EYE VIEW

Dear Stella,

My _____ was a lot more _____ before you came
      NOUN                          ADJECTIVE
along. Now you get all the _____, and I just have to stand here
                                NOUN
holding _____ and _____! Gloria hates me so much
         PLURAL NOUN      PLURAL NOUN
she hides me in (the) _____, and don't even get me started on
                       A PLACE
that _____.
      PERSON IN ROOM (MALE)
Please _____ away!
         VERB
Barkley


Dear Barkley,

Why don't you _____ me? I'm always very _____
                 VERB                              ADJECTIVE
to you—I clean your _____, and I never ever
                      PART OF THE BODY (PLURAL)
_____ on you. And as for _____—she hates
  VERB                           PERSON IN ROOM (FEMALE)
me, too! I used to have to jump into the swimming _____ to
                                                    NOUN
escape her, and she still blames me for her _____'s allergies.
                                              NOUN
Please be my _____!
              NOUN
Stella

From ADULT MAD LIBS®: Modern Family Mad Libs • TM & © 2016 Twentieth Century Fox Film
Corporation. Published by Price Stern Sloan, an imprint of Penguin Random House LLC,
345 Hudson Street, New York, NY 10014.

# MAD LIBS

**Download Mad Libs today!**

Join the millions of Mad Libs fans creating wacky and wonderful stories on our apps!